THE
WISDOM
OF
RUMI

A Guided Journal

Brimming with creative inspiration, how-to projects, and useful information to enrich your everyday life, Quarto Knows is a favorite destination for those pursuing their interests and passions. Visit our site and dig deeper with our books into your area of interest: Quarto Creates, Quarto Cooks, Quarto Homes, Quarto Lives, Quarto Drives, Quarto Explores, Quarto Gifts, or Quarto Kids.

This edition published in 2020 by Wellfleet Press,
an imprint of The Quarto Group,
142 West 36th Street, 4th Floor,
New York, NY 10018, USA
T (212) 779-4972 F (212) 779-6058
www.QuartoKnows.com

Contains content previously published as *The Love Poems of Rumi* in 2015 and 2020,
The Spiritual Poem of Rumi in 2018 and 2020, and *The Friendship Poems of Rumi* in 2020
by Wellfleet, an imprint of The Quarto Group, 142 West 36th Street, 4th Floor, New York, NY 10018, USA

Wellfleet titles are also available at discount for retail, wholesale, promotional, and bulk purchase.
For details, contact the Special Sales Manager by email at specialsales@quarto.com or by mail at The Quarto Group,
Attn: Special Sales Manager, 100 Cummings Center Suite 265D, Beverly, MA 01915 USA.

10 9 8 7 6 5 4 3 2 1

ISBN: 978-1-57715-238-5

Publisher: Rage Kindelsperger
Editorial Director: Pauline Molinari
Creative Director: Laura Drew
Managing Editor: Cara Donaldson
Project Editors: Leeann Moreau and Cathy Davis
Art Director: Cindy Samargia Laun
Book Design and Illustration: Evelin Kasikov

Poems compiled and edited by Dastan Khalili,
Sheefteh Khalili, Shiva Khalili, and Jessica Cauffiel

Printed in Singapore

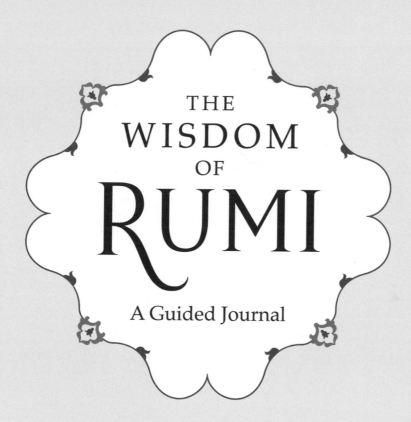

THE
WISDOM
OF
RUMI

A Guided Journal

Translated poems by Nader Khalili

WELLFLEET
PRESS

AN INTRODUCTION TO RUMI'S POETRY

Jalaloddin Mohammed Balkhi Rumi was born in 1207, in the city of Balkh, which is in present-day Afghanistan. He and his family fled from invading Mongols and settled in Konya—once a small town, it is now a major Turkish city. He lived the rest of his life there, studying languages, science, logic, and Islamic philosophy. He was a respected Islamic scholar and teacher on a steadfast course until the day he met great upheaval in the form of Shams Tabrizi, a Sufi Master who came to Konya in 1244.

Rumi was drawn to Shams, becoming his student and undergoing a profound transformation. The two spent an abundance of time together philosophizing and conversing until Shams was sent away to Syria, breaking Rumi's heart. Shams came back only to disappear again, this time forever, and this separation was to Rumi a manifestation of divine heartbreak. While he felt pain in separation, he took great joy from union. He knew that while he felt pained, he was never really separate from Shams or God. It was all this love, heartbreak, and longing that turned his soul to poetry.

In his life, he created 65,000 verses, many of which are robaiyat, or quatrains. His poems were recorded by his students as he recited them while whirling in the ecstatic dervish dance. The poetry was collected into two books, *Diwan-i Shams-I Tabrizi (The Collected Poetry of Shams)* and *Mathnawi (Spiritual Couplets)*.

Rumi remained a beloved and respected mystic throughout his life, and countless readers today consider him to be the very best Persian poet of his—or any—age. He reached what he called "the roots of the roots of the roots of the divine," meaning that his poetry captures a crucial aspect of Islam, and many other religions, which is that people can find bliss and freedom through pure love.

This collection of his poetry will inspire self-discovery and reflection, and is gathered from the nonliteral translations of Nader Khalili. The poems selected for this volume appear in four sections or themes which will guide you on your exploration of Rumi's mystical and inspirational words of poetry. Use the simple prompts in this interactive guided journal to explore and self-reflect on yourself and your world.

SPIRITUALITY

DON'T SEEK FAME

don't seek fame
as long as
you are not
secure in yourself
first wash your face
from fears
then show
your face

What have you been seeking that you shouldn't?

Write about a time you've experienced
sorrow and how you overcame it.

_____

_____

_____

_____

_____

_____

_____

_____

_____

_____

_____

_____

_____

_____

_____

AAH I SAID

aah i said
and my sigh
changed to a rope
and the rope hung
into the deep well i was in
i climb the rope
and out of the well
feeling happy giddy
and shining in face

i used to be desperate
at the bottom of the well
but now the whole world
can't contain my soul

bravo my dear God
all of a sudden
you separated me
from my sorrow

How do you see yourself?

_____

_____

_____

_____

_____

_____

_____

_____

_____

_____

_____

_____

COME AND SEE ME

come and see me
today i am away
out of this world
hidden away
from me and i

i grabbed a dagger
made slices of
me from myself
since i belong
not to me
not to anyone

i am so sorry
for not having done
this cutting away before
it was my soul's mind
and not mine

i have no idea
how my inner fire
is burning today
my tongue
is on a different flame

i see myself
with a hundred faces
and to each one
i swear it is me

surely i must have
a hundred faces
i confess none is mine
i have no face

EVERY MOMENT

every moment
a voice
out of this world
calls on our soul
to wake up and rise

this soul of ours
is like a flame
with more smoke than light
blackening our vision
letting no light through

lessen the smoke and
more light brightens your house
the house you dwell in now
and the abode
you'll eventually move to

now my precious soul
how long are you going to
waste yourself
in this wandering journey
can't you hear the voice
can't you use your swifter wings
and answer the call

What have you been ignoring?

_____

_____

_____

_____

_____

_____

_____

_____

_____

_____

_____

_____

_____

_____

_____

_____

_____

_____

_____

How does this poem inspire you?

IF YOU DON'T HAVE

if you don't have
enough madness in you
go and rehabilitate yourself

if you've lost a hundred times
the chess game of this life
be prepared to lose one more

if you're the wounded string
of a harp on this stage
play once more then resonate no more

if you're that exhausted bird
fighting a falcon for too long
make a comeback and be strong

you've carved a wooden horse
riding and calling it real
fooling yourself in life

though only a wooden horse
ride it again my friend
and gallop to the next post

you've never really listened
to what God has always
tried to tell you

yet you keep hoping
after your mock prayers
salvation will arrive

HOW LONG WILL
YOU HIDE

how long will you hide
your beautiful
festive smile

teach your laughter
to a flower
manifest an eternity

why do you think
the door to the sky
is closed on your face

it allures and invites
your magical touch
to open and arrive

an entire caravan
is waiting in ecstasy
for your coming and leading

come on my friend
use your talisman and
harness all their souls

today is the day to unite
with your longing beloved
wait no more
for an unknown tomorrow

a tambourine is in a corner
begging your playing hands
a flute is sitting dormant
begging your happy lips

What parts of yourself have you been hiding?

What kind of companion do you need?

_____

_____

_____

_____

_____

_____

_____

_____

_____

_____

_____

_____

_____

_____

I DON'T NEED

i don't need
a companion who is
nasty sad and sour

the one who is
like a grave
dark depressing and bitter

a sweetheart is a mirror
a friend a delicious cake
it isn't worth spending
an hour with anyone else

a companion who is
in love only with the self
has five distinct characters

stone hearted
unsure of every step
lazy and disinterested
keeping a poisonous face

the more this companion waits around
the more bitter everything will get
just like a vinegar
getting more sour with time

enough is said about
sour and bitter faces
a heart filled with desire for
sweetness and tender souls
must not waste itself with unsavory matters

DON'T BE BITTER
MY FRIEND

don't be bitter my friend
you'll regret it soon
hold to your togetherness
or surely you'll scatter

don't walk away gloomy
from this garden
you'll end up like an owl
dwelling in old ruins

face the war and
be a warrior like a lion
or you'll end up like a pet
tucked away in a stable

once you conquer
your selfish self
all your darkness
will change to light

Write about any bitterness you've been holding onto.

A VOICE OUT OF THIS WORLD

a voice out of this world
calls on our souls
not to wait any more
get ready to move
to the original home

your real home
your real birth place
is up here with the heavens
let your soul take a flight
like a happy phoenix

you've been tied up
your feet in the mud
your body roped to a log
break loose your ties
get ready for the final flight

make your last journey
from this strange world
soar for the heights
where there is no more
separation of you and your home

God has created
your wings not to be dormant
as long as you are alive
you must try more and more
to use your wings to show you're alive

these wings of yours
are filled with quests and hopes
if they are not used
they will wither away
they will soon decay

you may not like
what i'm going to tell you
you are stuck
now you must seek
nothing but the source

How have you been stuck?

WAKE UP MY
DEAR HEART

wake up my dear heart
the world is speeding away
your share of life
is being wasted away
don't just sleep in the body
or uselessly sit about
the caravan of life
is not waiting around

What dreams or ambitions do you have that you have been putting off?

_____

_____

_____

_____

_____

_____

_____

_____

_____

_____

What's something good you've done for someone?
Or what is something you can do for someone now?

GET UP AND DO SOME GOOD

get up and do some good
for someone now
the universe will surely
safekeep your act
everyone has left his
belongings and is gone
you too
except
for what good
you have done

Think about the people you surround yourself with.
How do the people in your life affect you?

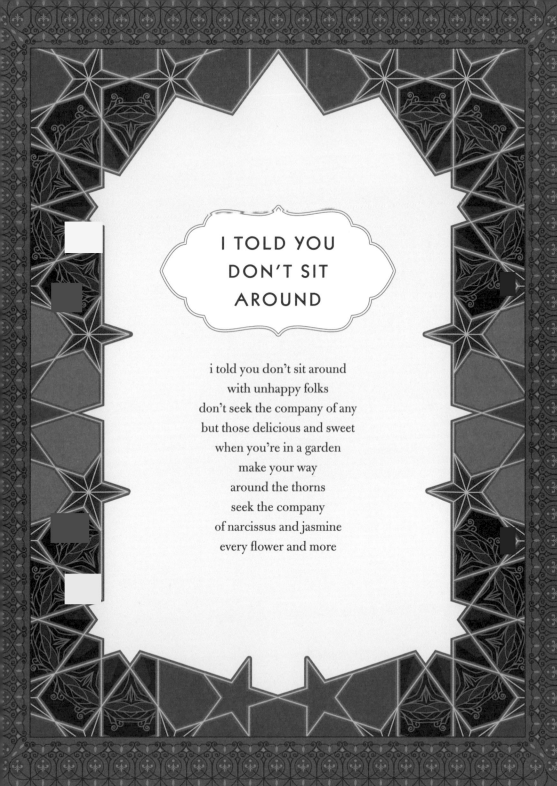

I TOLD YOU DON'T SIT AROUND

i told you don't sit around
with unhappy folks
don't seek the company of any
but those delicious and sweet
when you're in a garden
make your way
around the thorns
seek the company
of narcissus and jasmine
every flower and more

IF YOU DESIRE TO SEE

if you desire to see
eternal life
or discover wealth
in poverty
don't follow your path timidly
to discover real life
enter it like a hero

How does this inspire you?

THERE ARE TWO ATTITUDES

there are two attitudes
rendering us useless
two bad manners
chaining us for good
one
intoxication in self glory
the other
awakening coming too late

How do you relate to this?

_____

_____

_____

_____

_____

_____

_____

_____

_____

_____

_____

_____

_____

_____

_____

_____

What "idols" have you looked to
instead of yourself?

_____

_____

_____

_____

_____

_____

_____

_____

_____

_____

YOU MY
PEACEFUL PALS

you my peaceful pals
wandering around the world
why are you at a loss
searching for an idol
the one whom you're looking for
out in the world
if you search inside
you will find
you are the one

LOVE

ALL THE PRECIOUS WORDS

all the precious words
you and i have exchanged
have found their way
into the heart of the universe
one day they'll pour on us
like whispering rain
helping us arise
from our roots again

How does this make you feel?

What makes you happy?

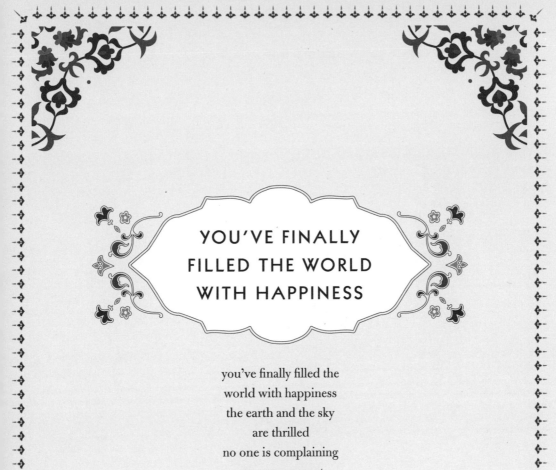

YOU'VE FINALLY FILLED THE WORLD WITH HAPPINESS

you've finally filled the
world with happiness
the earth and the sky
are thrilled
no one is complaining
any more except
the unhappiness
since you broke
everyone free
from its chains

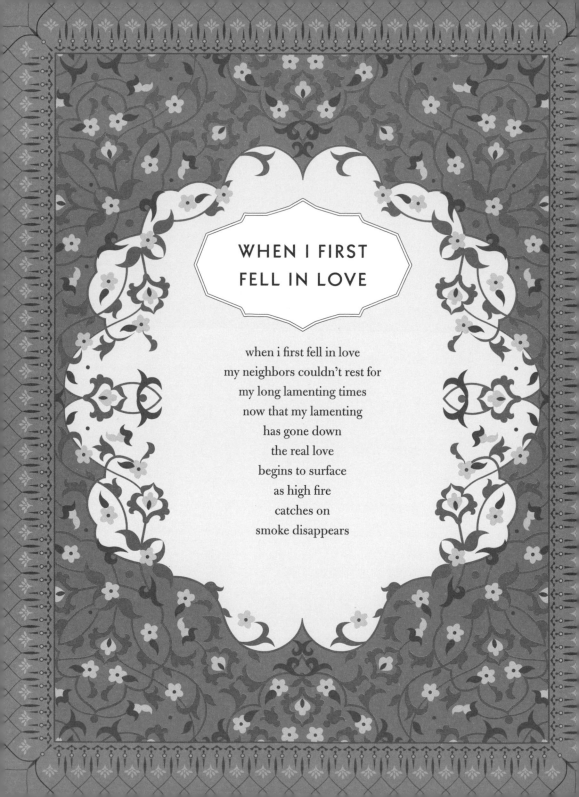

WHEN I FIRST
FELL IN LOVE

when i first fell in love
my neighbors couldn't rest for
my long lamenting times
now that my lamenting
has gone down
the real love
begins to surface
as high fire
catches on
smoke disappears

Write about the first time you fell in love.

_____

_____

_____

_____

_____

_____

_____

_____

_____

_____

_____

What is love to you?

LOVE IS

love is
what makes people happy
love is
what justifies our being
i was given birth by
the mother
who is called love
to that mother i bestow
a hundred blessings
a hundred cheers

I'LL LEAP HUNDRED STAGES

i'll leap hundred stages
beyond any wisdom
i'll break free
from all known good or bad
i have so much goodness
hidden inside
i'll finally fall in love
with no one but me

What do you love about yourself?

_____

_____

_____

_____

_____

_____

_____

_____

_____

_____

ALL THOSE IN LOVE ARE READY

all those in love are ready
to lose both worlds
in one stroke
let go of a
hundred years of life
in one day
travel a thousand miles
to experience a moment
and lose a thousand lives
for the sake of one heart

How do you relate to this?

What have you
learned about love?

_____

_____

_____

_____

_____

_____

_____

_____

_____

_____

SINCE I HAVE LEARNED

since i have learned
to love you
i've closed my eyes
to everyone
every flame
that love strikes
first catches on me
since i've been
scorched before

What's one of your favorite physical attributes of your significant other?

_____

_____

_____

_____

_____

_____

_____

_____

_____

_____

_____

_____

_____

_____

_____

I'M SO IN LOVE
WITH YOUR FACE

i'm so in love with your face
what do you think i should do
i'm shy to look at
your happy eyes
what do you think i should do
every moment
the pang of love
makes me scream
for God's sake
what do you think i should do

IF YOU'RE HAPPY

if you're happy
even for a moment
with your sweetheart
seize the moment
as the fulfillment
of your life
beware
let no breath
go to waste
since you will not find
that breath again

What are you most
grateful for about your significant other?

WITHOUT LOVE

without love
partying and good times
won't go very far
without love
human existence
won't elate and evolve
if a hundred drops of rain
fall from the clouds
over the sea
without the motion
of love
not one drop
can create a hidden
precious pearl

What would life be like without love?

_____

_____

_____

_____

_____

_____

_____

_____

_____

_____

_____

_____

_____

_____

_____

_____

_____

Have you ever loved someone so deeply that it changed you in some way? Describe how.

BELIEVE ME

believe me
i wasn't always like this
lacking common sense
or looking insane

like you
i used to be clever
in my days

never like this
totally enraptured
totally gone

like sharp shooters
i used to be
a hunter of hearts

not like today
with my own heart
drowning in its blood

nonstop asking and
searching for answers
that was then

but now
so deeply enchanted
so deeply enthralled

always pushing
to be ahead and above
since i was not yet hunted down
by this
ever-increasing love

IF YOU DWELL VERY LONG

if you dwell very long
in a heart depressed and dark
be aware you've fallen low
in will and quest

a heart filled with grief
whirling and spinning endlessly
can never feel at peace

what makes you
tremble in fear
that's your true worth now

whatever seems to be
your healing source
is the cause of your pain

whatever you think
is sure secure and forever
is what has hunted you down

whenever your mind flies
it can only land
in the house of madness

whenever love arrives
there is no space
for your self claim

a heart filled with love
is like a phoenix
that no cage can imprison

such a bird can only fly
above and beyond
any known universe

What have you been dwelling on?

LOOK AT LOVE

look at love
how it tangles
with one fallen in love

look at spirit
how it fuses with earth
giving it new life

why are you so busy
with this or that or good or bad
pay attention to how things blend

why talk about all
the known and the unknown
see how unknown merges into the known

why think separately
of this life and the next
when one is born from the last

look at your heart and tongue
one feels but deaf and dumb
the other speaks in words and signs

look at water and fire
earth and wind
enemies and friends all at once

the wolf and the lamb
the lion and the deer
far away yet together

look at the unity of this
spring and winter
manifested in the equinox

you too must mingle my friends
since the earth and the sky
are mingled just for you and me

be like sugarcane
sweet yet silent
don't get mixed up with bitter words

my beloved grows
right out of my own heart
how much more union can there be

Write down your thoughts on love.

If you have ever experienced heartbreak
reflect on it here. What helped you move on?

_____

_____

_____

_____

_____

_____

_____

_____

_____

_____

_____

_____

_____

_____

_____

MY DEAR FRIEND

my dear friend
never lose hope
when the beloved
sends you away

if you're abandoned
if you're left hopeless
tomorrow for sure
you'll be called again

if the door is shut
right in your face
keep waiting with patience
don't leave right away

seeing your patience
your love will soon
summon you with grace
rise you like a champion

and if all the roads
end up in dead ends
you'll be shown the secret paths
no one will comprehend

the beloved i know
will give with no qualms
to a puny ant
the Kingdom of Solomon

my heart has journeyed
many times around the world
but has never found
and will never find
such a beloved again

ah i better keep silence
i know this endless love
will surely arrive
for you and you and you

IF YOU CAN'T GO
TO SLEEP

if you can't go to sleep
my dear soul
for tonight
what do you think will happen

if you pass your night
and merge it with dawn
for the sake of heart
what do you think will happen

if the entire world
is covered with blossoms
you have labored to plant
what do you think will happen

if the elixir of life
that has been hidden in the dark
fills the desert and towns
what do you think will happen

if because of
your generosity and love
a few humans find their lives
what do you think will happen

if you pour an entire jar
filled with joyous wine
on the head of those already drunk
what do you think will happen

go my friend
bestow your love
even on your enemies
if you touch their hearts
what do you think will happen

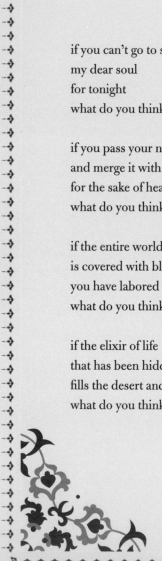

How does this poem inspire you to
share your love with others?

_____

_____

_____

_____

_____

_____

_____

_____

_____

_____

_____

_____

_____

_____

_____

_____

_____

FRIENDSHIP

FIND YOURSELF A FRIEND

find yourself a friend
who is willing to
tolerated you with patience

put to the test the essence
of the best incense
by putting it in fire

drink a cup of poison
if handed to you by a friend
when filled with love and grace

step into the fire
like the chosen prophet
the secret love will change
hot flames to a garden
covered with blossoms
roses and hyacinths and willow

spinning and throwing you
a true friend can hold you
like God and his universe

How would you describe a true friend?

COME ON SWEETHEART

come on sweetheart
lets' adore one another
before there is no more
of you and me

a mirror tells the truth
look at your grim face
brighten up and cast away
your bitter smile

a generous friend
gives life for a friend
let's rise above this
animalistic behavior
and be kind to one another

spite darkens friendships
why not cast away
malice from our heart

once you think of me
dead and gone
you will make up with me
you will miss me
you may even adore me

why be a worshipper of the dead
think of me as a goner
come and make up now

since you will come
and throw kisses
at my tombstone later
why not give them to me now
this is me
that same person

i may talk too much
but my heart is silence
what else can i do
i am condemned to live this life

What are some of your favorite memories with a best friend?

_____

_____

_____

_____

_____

_____

_____

_____

_____

_____

_____

_____

_____

_____

Describe a close friend and their best qualities here.

_____

_____

_____

_____

_____

_____

_____

_____

_____

_____

_____

_____

_____

_____

_____

_____

_____

WITHOUT
LOOKING AT YOU

without looking at you
i cannot touch the wine
without your hand
i cannot win the dice
you are asking me
to dance from afar
without your music
dance will not arrive

Which friend do you love to share
your time with and why?

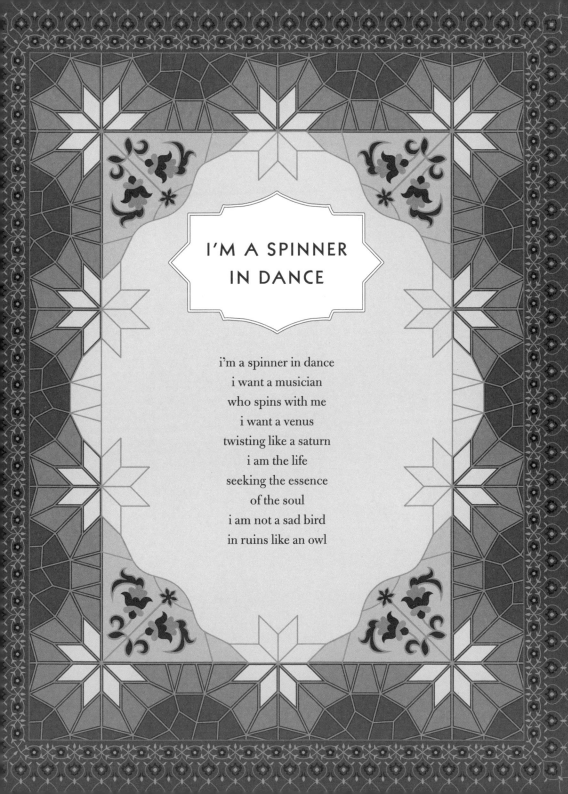

I'M A SPINNER
IN DANCE

i'm a spinner in dance
i want a musician
who spins with me
i want a venus
twisting like a saturn
i am the life
seeking the essence
of the soul
i am not a sad bird
in ruins like an owl

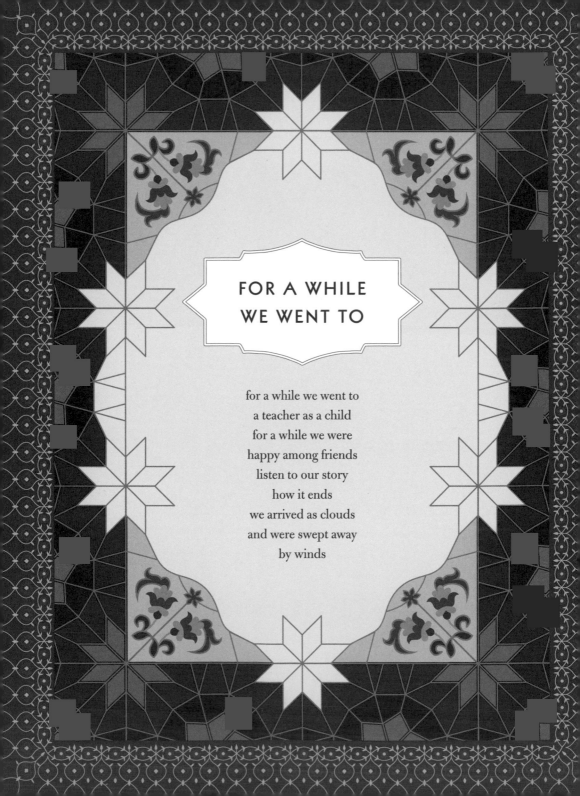

FOR A WHILE
WE WENT TO

for a while we went to
a teacher as a child
for a while we were
happy among friends
listen to our story
how it ends
we arrived as clouds
and were swept away
by winds

How does this poem make your feel?

_____

_____

_____

_____

_____

_____

_____

_____

_____

_____

_____

_____

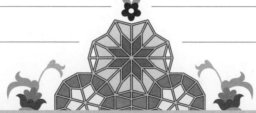

YOU CAN NEVER BREATHE

you can never breathe
healing to your body
till you cut off
worries from your breath
though you're weary at times
surely you can pull through

What words would you say to a
friend in need of moral support?

_____

_____

_____

_____

_____

_____

_____

_____

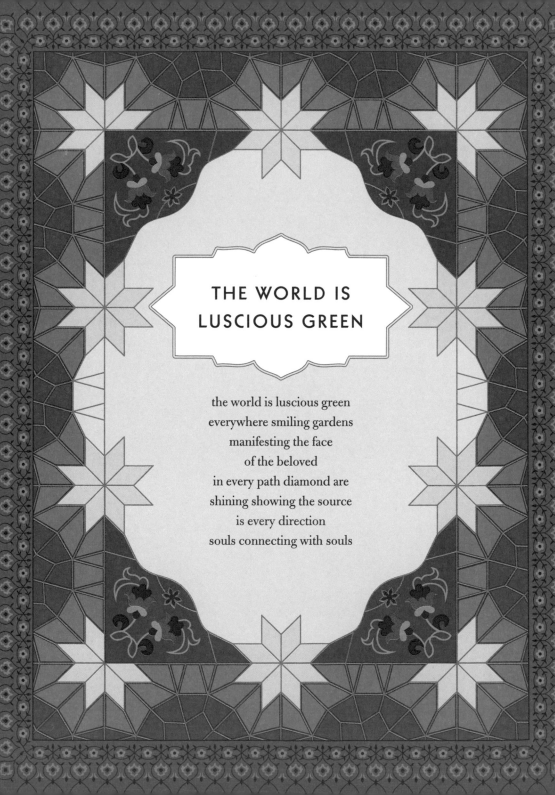

THE WORLD IS
LUSCIOUS GREEN

the world is luscious green
everywhere smiling gardens
manifesting the face
of the beloved
in every path diamond are
shining showing the source
is every direction
souls connecting with souls

How has your valued friendships made your life richer?

What are you grateful for when
thinking of your closest friend?

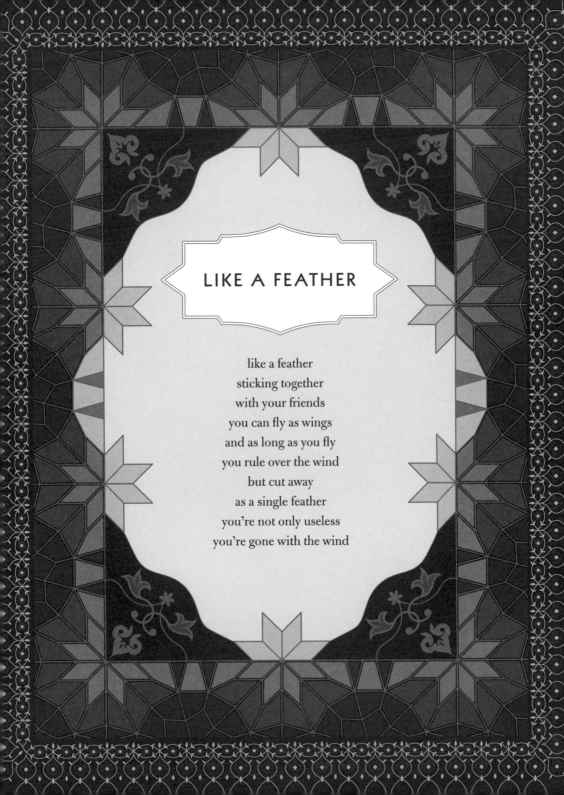

LIKE A FEATHER

like a feather
sticking together
with your friends
you can fly as wings
and as long as you fly
you rule over the wind
but cut away
as a single feather
you're not only useless
you're gone with the wind

How have you been vulnerable with others?

_____

_____

_____

_____

_____

_____

_____

_____

_____

_____

_____

_____

_____

_____

IN EVERY HEART
THERE IS

in every heart there is
a ray of your compassion
on every alter
there is a shedding of tears
one everlasting night
one glorious moonlight
i'll open to you the doors
to my longings
so far hidden in my heart

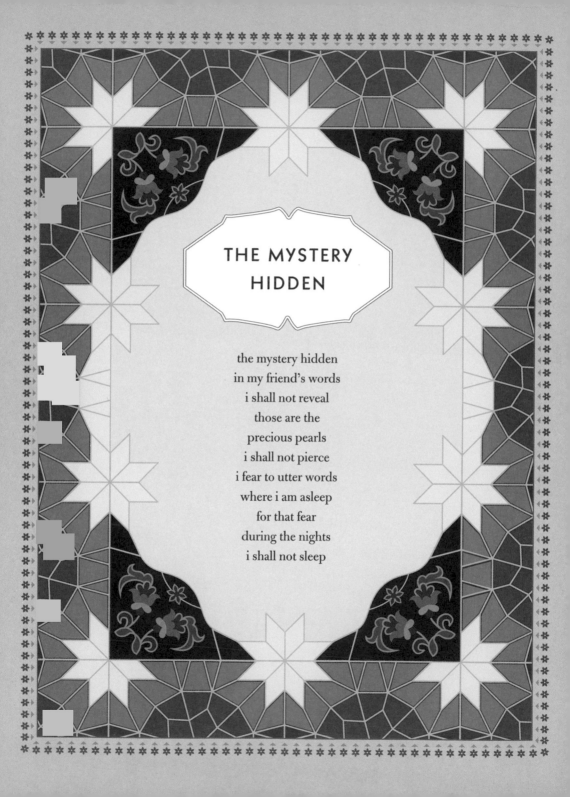

THE MYSTERY
HIDDEN

the mystery hidden
in my friend's words
i shall not reveal
those are the
precious pearls
i shall not pierce
i fear to utter words
where i am asleep
for that fear
during the nights
i shall not sleep

What does security with a friend mean to you?

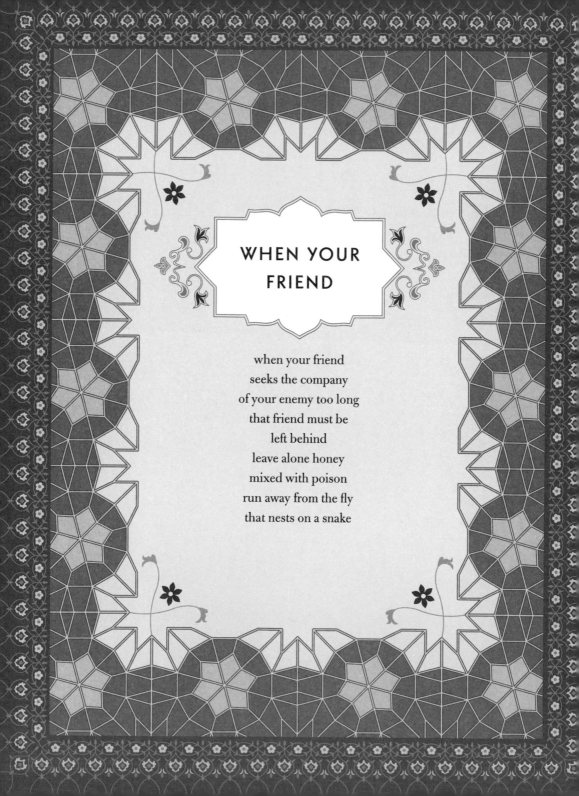

WHEN YOUR FRIEND

when your friend
seeks the company
of your enemy too long
that friend must be
left behind
leave alone honey
mixed with poison
run away from the fly
that nests on a snake

What qualities in a friend lift you up?

_____

_____

_____

_____

_____

_____

_____

_____

_____

_____

THE PAL
WITHIN YOU

the pal within you
the one who gives you breath
will also give hope
to reach your final quest
up to your last moment
take every breath
from the one inside
who is not playing with you
but generously
endows your every breath

Reflect on self-love here.

SELF-DISCOVERY

IF YOU DESIRE TO SEE

if you desire to see
eternal life
or discover wealth
in poverty
don't follow your path timidly
to discover real life
enter it like a hero

What big dreams do you have?

Meditate or find a quiet space and write down
what thoughts come to you here.

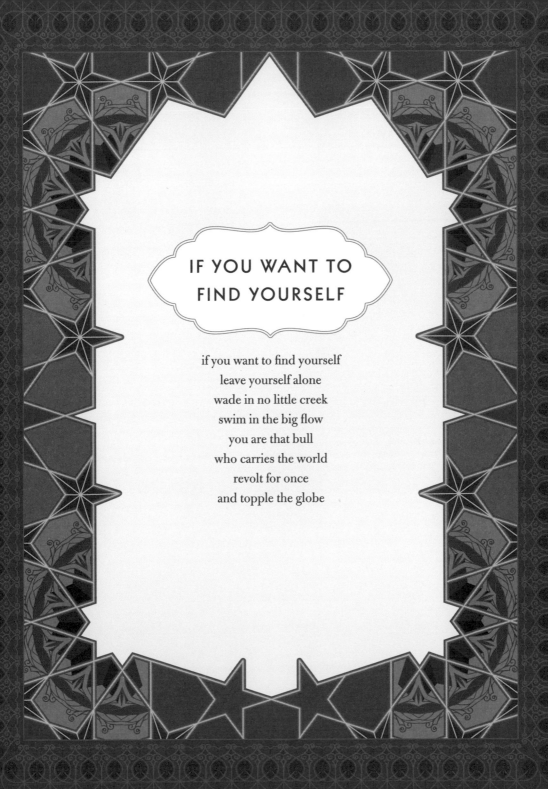

IF YOU WANT TO FIND YOURSELF

if you want to find yourself
leave yourself alone
wade in no little creek
swim in the big flow
you are that bull
who carries the world
revolt for once
and topple the globe

DON'T LOOK AT YOURSELF

don't look at yourself
how ugly or beautiful you are
look at your love (inside) instead
look at the one you love

Do you treat yourself as kindly as you treat others?

SEEK NOT WATER

seek not water
seek thirst
till you overflow
from the high and the low

What sparks your energy?

_____

_____

_____

_____

_____

_____

_____

_____

DON'T LOOK HOW

don't look how
low and weak you are
look at your aspiration instead

What have you achieved recently (no matter how small?)

_____

_____

_____

_____

_____

_____

_____

_____

THIS QUEST ITSELF
IS THE KEY

this quest itself is the key
to all your desires
this quest itself is the banner of
your victorious army

What do you feel most passionate about?

_____

_____

_____

_____

_____

_____

_____

_____

I AM HAPPY
WITH A WINE

i am happy with a wine
that has no cup
i shine every morning
and enjoy myself every night
they say you will
end up with nothing
i am happy
with no end at all

Where and/or when
do you feel most at peace?

What do you need to let go of?

CLEAR YOUR HEART FROM

clear your heart from
jealousy greed and grudge
uproot your bad habits
and bad thoughts
let go of denial
it causes your loss
welcome confession and
your profit will rise

I AM THE ONE
WITH HUNGER

i am the one with hunger
but have the happiness of
the one fulfilled
i am a fox who is
filled with lions
i have a self within
fearful of unknown dreams
but don't look at my fears
in essence i'm a brave soul

When are you in your best headspace?

_____

_____

_____

_____

_____

_____

_____

_____

_____

_____

_____

IF I ONLY KNEW

if i only knew
my own value
and perfection
i would pull out
of this lowly earth
evacuate myself
and rise to
soar my soul
to the ninth heaven

When do you feel the most confident?

How would you describe your
current level of self-belief?

_____

_____

_____

_____

_____

_____

_____

_____

_____

_____

HOW LONG WILL YOU WORRY

how long will you worry
about your poor little life
how long will you fret
this stinking world
all you will lose
is this one corpse
if one pile of rubbish
is gone
let go
so what

What can
lift your mood?

YOU HAVE
EYES TO SEE

you have eyes to see
the one who gives you
life and death
the one who makes you
laugh or depressed
that one is everywhere
from your toe to head

IF YOU CAN DISENTANGLE

if you can disentangle
yourself from your selfish self
all heavenly spirits
will stand ready to serve you

if you can finally hunt down
your own beastly self
you have the right
to claim Solomon's kingdom

you are that blessed soul who
belongs to the garden of paradise
is it fair to let yourself
fall apart in a shattered house

you are the bird of happiness
in the magic of existence
what a pity when you let
yourself be chained and caged

but if you can break free
from this dark prison named body
soon you will see
you are the sage and the fountain of life

What are you doing when you're in your perfect state of mind?

_____

_____

_____

_____

_____

_____

_____

_____

_____

_____

_____

_____

_____

Describe your perfect day.

_____

_____

_____

_____

_____

_____

_____

_____

_____

_____

IF YOU REACH FOR A STAR

if you reach for a star
you are a star
if you try
to make a living
you're merely bread
try to get this
secret message
as your last
you are what you seek
in your future
and the past

At what time of day do you feel mentally energized?
Use that time and space to visualize your goals and dreams.

THERE IS A SOUL

there is a soul
within your soul
seek it out
there is a treasure
in your mountain
seek it out
a mystic in motion
if that's what you are
don't seek out there
seek inside

DON'T SIT STILL

don't sit still
get up
hurry and
mingle now
a lazy body
either eats
or goes to sleep
there is the sound
of music and dance
in the air
move into the circle
of the enlightened
company now

When do you feel
the most connections or love?

SEEK ONLY THE KNOWLEDGE

seek only the knowledge
that unties the problems
of your life
seek it soon
before
your number is up
leave alone
what seems to be
but is not
seek what
seems not to be
yet it might

What are you most grateful for in your life?

_____

_____

_____

_____

_____

_____

_____

_____

_____

_____

_____

_____

_____

_____

ABOUT
THE TRANSLATOR

Nader Khalili (1936-2008) was a world-renowned
Iranian-American architect, author, humanitarian and teacher.
Khalili was also the founder and director of the California
Institute of Earth Art and Architecture (Cal-Earth).

Khalili was raised by the poetry of Rumi. As a child, his
grandmother would recite Rumi's poetry to lull him to sleep.
He later developed a passion for studying and translating
Rumi's works. Rumi's poetry also became an intrinsic part
of Khalili's architectural career. Inspired by the mystical
poetry of Rumi, his architecture was distilled from
the timeless principles of this universe and its timeless
materials—the elements of earth, air, water,
and fire, and has been described as
"Poetry crystallized into structure."